Michel de Ver

GW01090634

Celebrating Advent
Year C

the columba press

First published in 2000 by
the columba press
55A Spruce Avenue, Stillorgan Industrial Park,
Blackrock, Co Dublin

Cover by Bill Bolger
Origination by The Columba Press
Printed in Ireland by Colour Books Ltd, Dublin

ISBN 1 85607 309 2

Acknowledgements
Biblical quotations are from *The Jerusalem Bible,* copyright © Darton,
Longman and Todd and Doubleday and Company. Used by permission.

Contents

What is Advent?

This booklet, like those for Year A and B, is intended to help you celebrate Advent through meditation on the scripture passages which are prescribed for the Sundays of the season. One advantage of doing this is that you will be celebrating Advent in communion with the church, walking with millions of your fellow Christians who are following the same path, God's people in dialogue with him through his word.

However, you may have to modify your understanding of Advent, because in recent centuries it has been understood in a way that was wrong, or at least not in accord with the liturgy. Ask any group of Catholics what Advent is and nearly all will tell you that it is a time of preparation for Christmas. It is often taught like that at Mass or in school, where Christians are told that, just as they use these weeks to send greeting cards, buy decorations and presents, so they should go to confession and more frequent Masses to prepare themselves spiritually for the feast. But Advent *is a season in its own right* and with its own character which would exist even if there were no Christmas after it, and we must look at it in that light if we are to celebrate it with the church.

The Mystery of Waiting

Advent is the liturgical season when we pay special attention to the mystery of waiting. We have a real problem here because most of us don't like waiting, we don't see it as something to celebrate. In fact this may well be one of the reasons why people don't understand Advent correctly – although it may also be true that not celebrating it as we should has led us to misunderstand the value of waiting.

Whereas waiting bores and often irritates us, the bible teaches us that if we approach it in the right spirit, waiting is a creative moment when we grow spiritually. When we wait we are in touch with an essential aspect of our humanity which is

3

that we are dependent on God and on one another. It is also an act of love since, by waiting for others, we pay them the respect of letting them be free.

Waiting is a mystery – God waits and nature waits – so that when we as individuals wait we go beyond ourselves and enter into a sacred life-giving process, experiencing that we are made in the image and likeness of God. This is why Advent is a time of celebration. It is the season when we re-member with gratitude creative experiences of waiting in our lives or the lives of people we have known, the people who have waited for us at one time or another. We also remember the great waiting experiences in human history, in the bible, and especially in the life of Jesus.

But we must also make Advent a time of teaching. During this season all those involved in the work of Christian educ-ation, whether as catechists or preachers or guides, should explore the mystery of waiting: true and false ways of waiting, the danger of not knowing how to wait, ascetical practices that will help us wait more creatively.

Finally, waiting can be, as we know from our own experi-ence, a time of suffering and sometimes of despair. In Advent, we make a special effort to feel for those who are crying out in their agony, 'How long, O Lord?' – those we can name and the countless others 'whose faith is known to God alone'. Through our meditation we can let the special grace of the season flow through us to these brothers and sisters of ours, turning their mourning into dancing and their time of barren-ness into one of abundance and fertility.

The Readings for the
Sundays of Advent – Year C

The liturgy of the word is a teaching moment. It is not abstract teaching, where truths are presented to be learnt, but teaching by celebration. We celebrate biblical stories which exemplify the spirit of the particular season, identifying with the persons in them. In the process we learn more about biblical values, experience repentance as we become more aware of how we (and the whole church) have failed to practise those values, and pray that we will enter more fully into God's plan for us – that his kingdom will come. The main person we identify with is Jesus himself. At each liturgical season we celebrate one particular stage of his life on earth, not as a past event but as a way in which he continues to live among us.

The grace of Advent is hope, the virtue by which we human beings can recognise and welcome God present in the world but not experienced with our senses. The corresponding stage in Jesus' life which we celebrate in this season is when he was in the womb of Mary. It was a time in the history of salvation when the Word was made flesh, but was not visible, his presence was real but an object of hope, like the tiny mustard seed which we trust will eventually become a great tree in whose branches the birds of the air will shelter.

The fruit of Advent then is that we grow in the virtue of hope that God is present even when he is hidden. We are undaunted by evil, do not give up on our dreams, face with confidence the present historical moment (ours, that of our society and of the modern world), welcome the people he sends us, and help them get in touch with the best in themselves – where God is present.

In celebrating Jesus in the womb of Mary we celebrate all the times, in the bible and in history, when human beings have been invited by God to recognise his hidden presence in the world. The liturgical readings for the season then present us with biblical persons who are models of hope.

The bible teaches this through stories, not abstract defini-
tions. It does not attempt to define what hope is, but invites
us to meditate on people of hope. We celebrate them and
enter into their attitudes, how they interpreted the events of
their time and how they related to their contemporaries.

By doing this we celebrate our own experiences of hope, in
ourselves and others. In the process we experience conversion,
renew our hope which had grown cold. We also pray that
those in despair will turn to hope and we commit ourselves to
bringing hope into the world.

The prophets are the outstanding people of hope in the
bible, so we meditate on their writings during Advent – Isaiah
in years A and B, other prophets in this year C.

The texts convey the same basic message, but each Sunday
has its own emphasis, so that over the four weeks we get a
rounded picture of the person of hope.

This year's passages are attributed to various prophets who
lived between the eighth and seventh centuries BC; they were
composed at a much later period, however, when the Babylonian
exile was over and the people had returned to their own land
with great hopes of national renewal. The temple would be
rebuilt in its ancient glory, the monarchy would be restored.

These dreams did not materialise, however. Countless
obstacles stood in the way. Some came from outside, in the
form of enemies who were against the restoration of the Jewish
nation. Some came from within – the greed and corruption of
rulers. Besides, many remained in exile in different parts of
the world.

It was a time of disillusion and despair therefore and the
people returned to the writings of the great prophets so that
they could re-discover their message of hope. In addition they
inserted new texts into the old books, keeping the spirit of the
originals, but adapting them to their new situation. Our Advent
readings are a selection from these inserts, appropriately since
our time is much like that when they were composed. We too
return to ancient texts, 'inserting' our experience into them.

The following are the texts:
1st Sunday: Jeremiah – David's dynasty will be restored.
2nd Sunday: Baruch – the homecoming of exiles.
3rd Sunday: Zephaniah – the joy of hope.
4th Sunday: Micah – the Messiah King at the service of the world.
Gospels:
1st Sunday: 'Waiting for the Lord'.
2nd & 3rd Sundays: John the Baptist.
4th Sunday: Mary in her pregnancy.

How to use this book

The prayers proposed here are the fruit of *Lectio Divina,* a method of meditative bible reading which goes back to the early centuries of our church, and continues to be a source of deep spiritual growth. *Lectio Divina* (a Latin expression which means *Sacred Reading*) is done in three stages:
1. Reading: You read the passage slowly and reverently, allowing the words to sink into your consciousness. If necessary, you clarify the meaning of words or expressions that you are not familiar with.
2. Meditation: You allow the passage to stir up memories within you so that you recognise it in your own experience or that of people who have touched your life.
3. Prayer: You allow the meditation to lead you to prayer – thanksgiving, humility and petition.

The prayers given here are models. You may use them as they are, but they will also suggest ways in which you can pray from your own meditation. You will then be practising *Lectio Divina.*

We practice *Lectio Divina* most fruitfully when we do it in conjunction with the church's Sunday readings, spending the week with the readings for the following Sunday. By doing this, our personal prayer life becomes integrated into the prayer of the church, and reaches its high point each Sunday at the parish liturgy.

First Sunday of Advent

First Reading: Jeremiah 33:14-16
14See, the days are coming – it is the Lord who speaks – when I am going to fulfil the promise I made to the House of Israel and the House of Judah:
> *15'In those days and at that time,*
> *I will make a virtuous Branch grow for David,*
> *who shall practise honesty and integrity in the land.*
> *16In those days Judah shall be saved*
> *and Israel shall dwell in confidence.*
> *And this is the name the city will be called:*
> *The Lord-our-integrity.'*

Meditation

The first reading for this Sunday is one of the best known of the prophetic texts of the Old Testament.

The glorious destiny of the people is tied to the emergence of a great ruler. The people had been badly served by their rulers over the years; one after the other, they had betrayed the ideals of their ancestor David, the greatest of the kings of Israel, 'a man after God's own heart' as the tradition called him (e.g. Acts 13:22).

God had promised David a glorious dynasty; his descendants would be a luxuriant tree spreading its branches far and wide. The reality, however, was that the great tree had become a dried-up old stump. Yet their hope never died and now again the prophet speaks a word of hope. He looks at the stump, lifeless as it is, and proclaims with confidence that God will make a new branch spring from it.

As always with biblical hope, the prophet's confidence is based not on what he sees but on God's promise. His hope is the proclamation of God's will, to be realised through a human instrument.

This text is a teaching on hope then – the ability to look beyond the immediate and see the God-given potential in every person and community, in the human family itself.

Some of the language used in this passage is peculiar to the bible; you have to make the effort to understand the words so that you can turn the passage into your personal prayer.

Verse 14. 'The House of Israel and the House of Judah.' After David's death, the kingdom he had worked hard to unify tragically split into two warring factions, Israel in the north and Judah in the south. True believers always regretted this division and longed for a new David to restore unity to the nation. Today again, the prophetic word of hope is always that the longings of God's people are not disappointed. He will reconcile what sin and selfishness have divided.

Verse 15. The Jerusalem Bible translation 'virtuous' does not convey the full meaning of the original. It is the biblical concept of 'righteousness', meaning 'wholeness' or 'perfection', 'the harmonious blending of all the virtues'.

'Honesty and integrity' also mean wholeness, although 'honesty' reminds us that wholeness includes making just judgements.

It is significant that 'shall be saved' is parallelled with 'dwell in confidence'. In the bible 'salvation' includes 'dwelling in confidence'.

Verse 16. 'This is the name the city will be called' is a biblical way of saying that this is the people's destiny, the potential within them, the object of our hope.

'The Lord-our-integrity' means that the people's wholeness is 'grace', a sharing in God's wholeness or perfection. Integrity is not theirs but a gift they receive humbly from the hands of God.

Prayer

'I believe that unarmed truth and unconditional love will have the final word in reality.' *Martin Luther King, receiving the Nobel Peace Prize.*

Lord, many today don't see any hope for our civilisation or for humanity.

We are as in the return from exile when your people looked in vain for a leader who would bring them back to their greatness.

Like them, we remember the promise of earlier days:

* the age of liberty, equality and fraternity
* the war to end all wars
* the end of colonialism when all nations would be free and independent.

What we hoped would be a luxuriant tree with spreading branches under which your people would find shade, has become nothing but a dried-up stump.

We thank you that you always send us your prophets to renew our hope.

Jeremiah re-assured the people that from the dried-up stump you would raise a virtuous branch for David, who would practise honesty and integrity in the land, and that under his leadership Judah would be saved and Israel dwell in confidence.

Jesus told his contemporaries that they could stand erect and hold their heads high because their liberation was near at hand.

In our time too, you send us great men and women to rekindle our hope, not primarily by their words but by the way they practice honesty and integrity on the earth:

* Martin Luther King dreamt of a nation where there would be racial harmony;
* Mother Teresa brought your tenderness into areas of indifference;
* Archbishop Romero preached love and compassion in a country torn by civil strife.

Like Jeremiah and Jesus, they tell us that new beginninga are always possible, that you will fulfil your promises and make a virtuous branch grow for David; our civilisation can be saved, humanity can dwell in confidence.

They invite us to dream of a world where all divisions are reconciled, called not a culture of death but a civilisation of love, a city of harmony and wholeness, not the fruit of human endeavour but gratefully received as a sharing in your divine life.

'The tourists see in us about ten yards of sand and a Margarita. They take a break from the empire's problems and spend 14 days.' *Caribbean poet, Derek Walcott.*

Lord, many people today come to others looking for what they can get from them:
- visit tourist resorts only to enjoy sea and sand;
- look on third world countries as an investment;
- give hand-outs to the poor instead of working to eradicate poverty.

Help us to come to every person and culture with deep respect, so that we can discover their true names – your people, your creation, your wholeness and harmony.

Gospel Reading: Luke 21:25-28, 34-36

Jesus said to his disciples: 25*'There will be signs in the sun and moon and stars; on earth nations in agony, bewildered by the clamour of the ocean and its waves;* 26*men dying of fear as they await what menaces the world, for the powers of heaven will be shaken.* 27*And then they will see the Son of Man coming in a cloud with power and great glory.* 28*When these things begin to take place, stand erect, hold your heads high, because your liberation is near at hand.'*

34*'Watch yourselves, or your hearts will be coarsened with debauchery and drunkenness and the cares of life, and that day will be sprung on you suddenly, like a trap.* 35*For it will come down on every living man on the face of the earth.* 36*Stay awake, praying at all times for the strength to survive all that is going to happen, and to stand with confidence before the Son of Man.'*

Meditation

The gospel readings for Advent each year invite us to meditate on the mystery of waiting, and they do it by presenting us with stories of great people who knew how to wait.

On the first Sunday, Jesus himself is the model as he taught his followers the spirituality of 'waiting in joyful hope'.

The passage is clearly in two sections, verses 25 to 28, and 34 to 36.

You must interpret verses 25 to 28 in the light of your experience, times when your world or the world of your family or other community collapsed. Allow the dramatic language to express this experience, making sure that you recognise the double movement of collapse and re-birth.

If you decide to meditate on verses 34 to 36, the key will be to identify concretely the meaning of 'that day', a time like the one in verses 25 to 28. Then you will get a feel for the teaching of Jesus.

Prayer

Lord, great tragedies befall us from time to time:
  * we lose our job;
  * a spouse proves unfaithful;
  * we discover that one of our children is on drugs;
  * we fall into a sin we thought we had overcome.

These are moments of great distress. It is as if the sun and moon and stars are no longer there in the heavens. We feel as if we are drowning, the ocean and its clamorous waves overwhelming us. The powers of heaven have been shaken and we are dying of fear as we await the future which menaces us.

But, somehow or other, that moment, terrible as it is, brings its own grace:
  * we find we have more courage than we thought;
  * our family finds a new unity;
  * we forgive a long-standing hurt.

Jesus comes into our lives with power and great glory.

We have learnt now that we need never panic.

When these things begin to take place, we can stand erect, hold our heads high, because a moment of grace and liberation is near at hand.

'It was a time when we felt happy and proud to be Haitians.' *President Aristide, reflecting on his presidency, November 1991.*

Lord, we thank you for the times when oppressed people can stand erect and hold their heads high because a moment of liberation is near at hand.

'After one time, is two time.' *Trinidad saying.*

Lord, at one point in our lives we felt that good times would never end. We lived mindlessly, looking down on others who were less successful or less virtuous. We thank you for bringing us to our senses:
  * we fell sick;
  * we fell into a sin we thought we would never commit;
  * one of our children got into trouble with the law.

It was Jesus warning us to watch ourselves, and reminding us that the day of reckoning is always sprung on us like a trap, for it comes down on every living person on the face of the earth.

Lord, make us aware of how our minds have been coarsened by over-indulgence and being too much engrossed by the cares of this life.
We know that what counts in life is to be able to stand with confidence before the Son of Man.

Lord, we sometimes think that, as a church community, we are exempt from the ups and downs of institutions.
But the day of crisis is sprung on us suddenly like a trap, just as it comes down on every group on the face of the earth.

Second Sunday of Advent

First Reading: Baruch 5:1-9

[1]Jerusalem, take off your dress of sorrow and distress,
put on the beauty of the glory of God for ever,
[2]wrap the cloak of the integrity of God around you,
put the diadem of the glory of the Eternal on your head:
[3]since God means to show your splendour to every nation   under
*   heaven,*
[4]since the name God gives you for ever will be,
'Peace through integrity, and honour through devotedness'.
[5]Arise, Jerusalem, stand on the heights
and turn your eyes to the east:
see your sons reassembled from west to east
at the command of the Holy One, jubilant that God has
*   remembered them.*
[6]Though they left you on foot,
with enemies for an escort,
now God brings them back to you
like royal princes carried back in glory.
[7]For God has decreed the flattening
of each high mountain, of the everlasting hills,
the filling of the valleys to make the ground level
so that Israel can walk in safety under the glory of God.
[8]And the forests and every fragrant tree will provide shade
for Israel at the command of God;
[9]for God will guide Israel in joy by the light of his glory
with his mercy and integrity for escort.

Meditation

The biblical character Baruch first appears in the Book of Jeremiah. He was the prophet's confidant, man of business and scribe. Jer 36:4 relates, 'Jeremiah summoned Baruch, son of Neriah, who at his dictation wrote down on the scroll all the words the Lord has spoken to him.'

The book attributed to Baruch, however, is by an anonymous author of the post-exilic period. Jerusalem in this passage represents God's people in every age, longing to attain the wholeness that is their destiny. The prophetic word is that God will fulfil this longing – 'blessed are they who mourn, they shall be comforted' (Mt 5:5).

The language is poetic, the basic image being of a mother welcoming back her lost children. She was humiliated to see them depart in disgrace; now she sees them returning home as princes and princesses.

Verses 1-4. The change of status reflected in a change of garments. A humble person ('your dress of sorrow and distress') is clothed in robes that are both royal and priestly (the 'diadem of the glory of the Eternal' refers to the 'mitre' worn by the High Priest).

'Peace through integrity and honour through devotedness.' As in last Sunday's reading, this is the biblical ideal of wholeness. The inner dispositions ('integrity' and 'devotedness') are reflected externally ('peace' and 'honour'). 'Devotedness' means 'humble worship' – true wholeness includes harmony with God, like Adam walking with God in the cool of the day (Gen 3:8).

Verses 5-9. The prophet invites the Holy City to stand on its parapets and welcome back her children.

V 5. We think of the father of the prodigal son keeping watch so that he sees the son 'while he was still a long way off' (Lk 15:20).

V 6. They left on foot, like prisoners of war, heads bowed, escorted by their captors; now they are carried like royalty on portable thrones.

V 7. The filling of valleys and the flattening of hills represent the tumbling down of all obstacles – like the walls of Jericho falling at the sound of Joshua's trumpets (Jos 6:5).

V 8. The desert blooms. Miraculous rain causes forest trees to grow and spread luxuriant branches.

V 9. Mercy and integrity are divine attributes; the image is as in the Good Shepherd psalm, 'goodness and kindness shall follow me all the days of my life'.

Prayer

Lord, we remember times when we felt weak and vulnerable:
* a project we had set our hearts on failed;
* we fell into a sin we never thought we would commit;
* a social movement we had great hopes for collapsed;
* our church community was torn apart by scandal.

We were like a mother seeing her children defeated and sent into exile. But then you sent your messenger who lifted our spirits – a teacher, a friend, one of our parents or grandparents, a counsellor, a priest in confession, a national leader.

They told us we could take off our dress of sorrow and distress, and put on the beauty of the glory of God forever; we could wrap the cloak of God's integrity around us and put the diadem of his glory on our heads; you would show our splendour to every nation under heaven.

We felt ashamed, but they gave us a new name that would be with us for ever, peace through integrity and honour through devotedness.

We felt we had accomplished nothing, but they told us to arise, stand on the heights, turn our eyes to the east and see our children reassembled from west and east at the command of the Holy One, jubilant that you had remembered us.

The dreams we had for ourselves had collapsed, sent into exile like the Israelites on foot with bowed heads, escorted by enemies, but now we saw them coming to fulfilment, brought home like royalty carried in glory.

Every way forward had seemed blocked; now we realised that you had decreed the flattening of each high mountain, of the everlasting hills, the filling of valleys to make the ground level, so that we could walk in safety under your glory.

We were now as in a beautiful forest, where every fragrant tree provided shade for us at your command.

We were no longer lost, you were guiding us in joy by the light of your glory, with your mercy and your integrity for our escorts.

'I have a dream that one day this nation will rise up and live out the true meaning of its creed, "We hold these truths to be self-evident, that all people are created equal".' *Martin Luther King.*

Lord, like Irael. all peoples come into being with the high ideal of living together as brothers and sisters, but then allow themsdelves to be torn apart by greed and the desire for power so that some of their members are alienated and dispersed.

At this time in history, some memnbers of the human family have fallen into this trap:
 * the Republic of the Congo;
 * Sri Lanka;
 * former Yugoslavia;
 * Haiti;
 * Peru.
Send them prophetic leaders who will challenge them
 * to take off their dress of sorrow and distress and put on the beauty of your glory for ever,
 * to wrap the cloak of your integrity around them and put the diadem of your glory on their head,
 * leaders who will remind them that their destiny is to show their splendour to every nation under heaven, and will command them to stand above their prejudices, turn their eyes away from past quarrels and turn rather to the east so that they can welcome all their sons and daughters reassembled from east and west,
 * jubilant that they are no longer treated with suspicion and escorted by guards, but are carried on thrones like royalty.
Then their countries will no longer be deserts but luxuriant forests providing shade for all their citizens and they will be guided by your mercy and integrity.

'The task of the modern educator is not to cut down jungles but to irrigate deserts.' *C. S. Lewis.*

Lord, we thank you for teachers who give a sense of self-

worth to their students, take off their dress of sorrow and distress and wrap them in a cloak of integrity, put a diadem of
glory on their heads, and show their splendour to the world.

Commendation of the Dying
Dear Sister/Brother,
In the name of the Lord Jesus, we invite you to enter into
     God's glory.
Take off your dress of sorrow and distress,
put on the beauty of the glory of God for ever,
wrap the cloak of eternal life around you,
put the diadem of his eternal glory on your head.
God is about to show your splendour to the angels and saints.
He will call you by a new name, peace through integrity and
     devotion through devotedness.
You walked the earth like someone banished into exile,
     escorted by your enemies;
now the angels are bringing you home, like royalty carried in
     glory.
As you face these final moments on your way to God's
     glorious kingdom, may the mountains of fear be flattened,
the valleys of anxiety filled in to make the ground level,
forests and fragrant trees provide shade for you
and God himself guide you in joy, by the light of his glory,
with his mercy and his salvation for your escort.

Gospel Reading: Luke 3:1-6

¹*In the fifteenth year of Tiberius Caesar's reign, when Pontius Pilate was governor of Judaea, Herod tetrarch of Galilee, his brother Philip tetrarch of the lands of Ituraea and Trachonitis, Lysanias tetrarch of Abilene, ²during the pontificate of Annas and Caiaphas, the word of God came to John son of Zechariah, in the wilderness. ³He went through the whole Jordan district proclaiming a baptism of repentance for the forgiveness of sins, ⁴as it is written in the book of the sayings of the prophet Isaiah:*

A voice cries in the wilderness:
Prepare a way for the Lord,
make his paths straight.
⁵*Every valley will be filled in,*
every mountain and hill be laid low,
winding ways will be straightened
and rough roads made smooth.
⁶*And all mankind shall see the salvation of God.*

Meditation

On the second and third Sundays of Advent, the church gives us John the Baptist as a model of someone who knows how to wait.

In this first passage we have Luke's summary of the mission of John the Baptist. It is none other than the mission of Jesus himself and of all preachers of the gospel.

In verses = 1 and 2 St Luke invites us to meditate on God's word, bypassing the powerful ones of the world and coming to John in the wilderness.

Verse 3 is a concise summary of John's (and Jesus') preaching.

There are two aspects to verses 4 and 5: the fact that John lived out the vocation of Isaiah, and then the content of his preaching expressed in poetic language. We are invited to identify with both aspects.

Prayer

'I thank you, Father, for hiding these things from the learned and the clever and revealing them to mere children.' *Luke 10:21.*

Lord, we forget your way of doing things. We think it is important to seek the favour of the great ones of the world, as if their patronage is necessary for the spread of your gospel, while we neglect the wisdom of the poor.

But your word has always bypassed
* Tiberius Caesar reigning for 15 years;
* Pilate, the great governor;
* those powerful tetrarchs Herod, Philip and Lysanius;
and come to a humble person, living in the wilderness.

Lord, we remember a time when we were in the wilderness:
* our family relationships were at their lowest level;
* at work everything seemed to be going wrong;
* violence and crime ruled in the country;
* our prayer life was as dry as dust.
Yet within that very wilderness there was a voice within us, crying out that things would turn out right.

We felt so sure of this that, even in the midst of all that desolation, we prepared a way for your coming and made the paths straight so that we would be there to welcome you. We saw some deep valleys and wondered how we would ever get across them, but we knew that every one of them would be filled in. There were high mountains before us; they would all be laid low. The road was winding, so that every time we turned a corner another one appeared; it would be straightened. As for the rough roads that had our feet sore and bleeding, they would become smooth as glass. We knew for sure that we would experience your salvation. Thank you, Lord.

'We live in a world where no one cares.' *School principal, The Express, 10 November 1991.*

Lord, we pray that in our heartless world the church may,

like John the Baptist, fulfil what is written in the book of the sayings of the prophet Isaiah, and be a voice crying out to those who feel themselves in a wilderness that you have not abandoned them, that every valley will be filled in, every mountain and hill laid low, winding ways will be straightened and rough roads made smooth.

'If all people are God's children, why are we rejoicing when our sons and daughters were safe while death and destruction were wreaked upon innocent people?' *Religious Superiors of the USA after the Gulf War.*

Lord, we still need John the Baptist to teach us your will that all must see your salvation.

'A critical ingredient of the Caribbean today is collective self-knowledge as the vital pre-condition to collective self-possessiveness.' *Lloyd Best.*

Lord, give us the grace to know that what we are doing is written in the books of the sayings of the prophets.

Third Sunday of Advent

First Reading: Zephaniah 3:14-18

¹⁴*Shout for joy, daughter of Zion,*
Israel, shout aloud!
Rejoice, exult with all your heart,
daughter of Jerusalem!
¹⁵*The Lord has repealed your sentence;*
he has driven your enemies away.
The Lord, the king of Israel, is in your midst;
you have no more evil to fear.
¹⁶*When that day comes, word will come to Jerusalem:*
Zion, have no fear,
do not let your hands fall limp.
¹⁷*The Lord your God is in your midst,*
a victorious warrior.
He will exult with joy over you,
he will renew you by his love;
he will dance with shouts of joy for you
¹⁸*as on a day of festival.*

Meditation

This Sunday's passage teaches that true hope leads to joy.

Joy is a frequent theme in the bible, Old and New Testaments. Jesus told his followers, 'I have told you this so that my own joy may be in you and your joy be complete.' St Paul often exhorts his Christians to 'rejoice always'. At each Mass we celebrate that 'we wait in joyful hope'.

The passage teaches us to understand our 'joyful hope' correctly. At the time it was written, the people were disillusioned, fearful for the future, conscious of their enemies around them preventing them from attaining their great destiny. It is in this situation that the prophet invites them to be joyful.

True hope avoids two false paths therefore. It is not naïve; the victory has not been won, there is still evil in the world. Our hope is based not on positive signs we have seen but on

God. We know we have a 'victorious warrior in our midst'.

Jesus lived this hope on the night before his passion. He knew that Judas had betrayed him and that he was about to be arrested, but he said to the apostles, 'I shall not talk with you any longer because the prince of this world is on his way; he has no power over me' (Jn 14:30).

The tenses of our passage are instructive:

* In verse 15 the verbs are in the perfect tense, 'has repealed', 'has driven'.

* In verses 17 and 18 they are in the future, 'he will exult', 'he will renew'.

We are so certain that God's promises will be fulfilled that we can celebrate them as having already happened. It is also true that when we hope we have already conquered. Again on that final night when Jesus was powerless against his enemies, he assured his disciples, 'in the world you will have trouble but be brave, I have conquered the world' (Jn 16:33).

The atmosphere of our passage is not merely joyful but ecstatic. Hope is like a convicted prisoner whooping it up because he has just heard that his sentence is repealed; like citizens singing and dancing in the streets the whole night long when the enemy army has been driven away from the national territory; like a prince letting himself go at a disco, or a proud father dancing with his daughter at her wedding feast.

Some may find it difficult to identify with these images at a time of sorrow. The language is hyperbolic as often in the bible. 'If any one would have your tunic, let him have your cloak as well' (Mt 5:39); 'If any one comes to me without hating father, mother, wife, children, brothers, sisters, he cannot be my disciple' (Lk 14:26); 'Take nothing for the journey except a staff, no bread, no haversack, no coppers for your purses' (Mk 6:8).

We must get to the spirit of the images and recognise how they correspond to our experience. They convey something very important which is that people of hope don't feel sorry for themselves, they don't suffer from 'victim syndrome'.

They are energetic, life-giving, good humoured; they bring joy to those around them.

Jesus captured this joy in the midst of persecution when he exhorted his followers, 'Happy are you when people hate you, drive you out, abuse you, denounce your name as criminal on account of the Son of Man. Rejoice when that day comes and dance for joy, for then your reward will be great in heaven. This was how your ancestors treated the prophets' (Lk 6:23).

This comes out in the story of Fr Maximilian Kolbe. He was in one of the Nazi concentration camps during World War II and volunteered for the death chamber in the place of one of his fellow prisoners. The jailers reported that whereas the death chambers were usually places of despair and cursing, in this case the condemned men were singing hymns.

When Archbishop Romero was asked by a newspaper reporter if he was aware that people were out to kill him, he replied, 'You can tell them they're wasting their time. They can kill a bishop but they cannot kill the people of God, the church. If I am killed I will rise again in the people of El Salvador.'

Those who were arrested during the civil rights and other dissident movements often turned their prisons into places of joy.

The prophet invites people to enter into that kind of hope.

Prayer
'The slaves have wrested God from their captors.' *Derek Walcott.*

Lord, we thank you for those who remain strong in times of failure or rejection:
* people of prayer, self-possessed even when they do not know what to do;
* victims of racial or cultural prejudice who maintain their dignity;
* families remaining united when one of their parents has deserted them;
* non-violent dissidents.

They shout for joy, shout aloud, rejoice and exult with all their hearts.

They are sentenced by their fellow human beings but you repeal the sentence.

They are surrounded by enemies, but drive away feelings of fear or resentment.

They know that you, the Lord, the king of Israel, are in their midst, and they have no more evil to fear.

On that day, your word comes to them that they need have no fear, and need not let their hands fall limp.

You are in their midst, a victorious warrior.

They are mocked and threatened but are untouched; they know that you are exulting with joy over them and renewing them by your love; you are dancing with shouts of joy for them, as on a day of festival.

'The church has proclaimed herself the handmaid of humanity.'
Pope Paul VI

Lord, forgive us for the times that, as your church, we have approached other cultures with a sense of superiority, focusing on their faults.

Help us to approach all who differ from us with admiration, to proclaim that they are blessed, that they must shout for joy and shout aloud, rejoice and exult with all their hearts, because you are in their midst like a victorious warrior, you exult with joy over them and renew them by your love, dance with shouts of joy for them, as on a day of festival.

Gospel Reading: Luke 3:10-18

[10]*When all the people asked John, 'What must we do?'* [11]*he answered, 'If anyone has two tunics he must share with the man who has none, and the one who has something to eat must do the same.'* [12]*There were tax collectors too who came for baptism, and these said to him, 'Master, what must we do?'* [13]*He said to them, 'Exact no more than your rate.'* [14]*Some soldiers asked him in their turn, 'What about us? What must we do?' He said to them, 'No intimidation! No extortion! Be content with your pay!'*

[15]*A feeling of expectancy had grown among the people, who were beginning to think that John might be the Christ,* [16]*so John declared before them all, 'I baptise you with water, but someone is coming, someone who is more powerful than I am, and I am not fit to undo the strap of his sandals; he will baptise you with the Holy Spirit and fire.* [17]*His winnowing fan is in his hand to clear his threshing floor and to gather the wheat into his barn; but the chaff he will burn in a fire that will never go out.'* [18]*As well as this, there were many other things he said to exhort the people and announce the Good News to them.*

Meditation

On the third Sunday St Luke gives us a glimpse into the personality of that wonderful person, John the Baptist. In your meditation, let him remind you of great people you have known.

In verses 10 to 14 John speaks openly. Notice how he has a different word for each group which questions him. Notice too how the soldiers feel that even they can get a word of salvation.

Verses 15 to 18 give us a further insight into the kind of person John the Baptist was. He may have said these words in a moment of discouragement, in which case they express his trust that God would complete what was lacking in his ministry. But perhaps they tell us of his humility in the midst of his extraordinary success as a preacher.

Prayer

'The bread you do not use is the bread of the hungry.' *St Ambrose.*

Lord, we thank you for people who are direct and honest like John the Baptist. When we ask them what we must do, they don't beat around the bush but tell us openly: those who have two tunics must share with those who have none, and those with something to eat must do the same.

Lord, John the Baptist knew his people. When the tax collectors came for baptism he told them exactly what they must do, and so too with the soldiers.

Lord, we pray for the church today.

'We all want to be famous people, but the moment we want to be something we are no longer free.' *Krishnamurti.*

Lord, give us the humility of John the Basptist. When a feeling of expectancy grows and our followers begin to think that we might be some kind of Messiah, help us to declare before them all that we are merely baptising with water. There is one who is more powerful than we are and he baptises with the Holy Spirit and with fire.

'We are a resourceful people but deadly scared of our own natively-inspired success.' *Clifford Sealey, Trinidadian poet, died September 1991.*

Lord, often we do not accomplish what we can because we are afraid of failure. We must be content to baptise with water, trusting that someone will come after us who is more powerful than we are, and he will baptise with the Holy Spirit and with fire.

'Something happened between me and the earth. The land recognised me.' *Earl Lovelace as he landed on African soil for the first time, November 1991.*

Lord, we thank you for the moments of grace when we feel we are connected with the whole of creation and all of our history. We know then that your winnowing fan is in your hand, that evil is merely chaff which you will burn in a fire that will never go out, whereas we are your precious wheat which you will gather into your barn.

Fourth Sunday of Advent

First Reading: Micah 5:1-4

The Lord says this:
¹You, Bethlehem Ephrathah,
the least of the clans of Judah,
out of you will be born for me
the one who is to rule over Israel;
his origin goes back to the distant past,
to the days of old.
²The Lord is therefore going to abandon them
till the time when she who is to give birth gives birth.
Then the remnant of his brothers will come back
to the sons of Israel.
³He will stand and feed his flock
with the power of the Lord,
with the majesty of the name of his God.
They will live secure, for from then on he will extend his power
to the ends of the land.
⁴He himself will be peace.

Meditation

The passage for this fourth Sunday teaches us that Christian hope is not self-centred. We hope for greatness not for our own sakes, but so that we can serve others.

Similarly our hope for others is that they will fulfil their destiny to be creative members of the community.

As with the preceding Sundays, the context of this passage is gloomy. We capture the atmosphere in the preceding verse: 'They have laid siege against us; with a rod they strike on the cheek the judge of Israel.' The situation is not merely perilous but humiliating – the judiciary is a crucial institution to the dignity of a society; here the enemies 'strike the judge of Israel on the cheek'. In this situation, the prophet picks out the 'least of the clans of Judah' and sees that they have a glorious destiny.

As on the first Sunday the image is of a new David. The prophet goes back to 'the distant past, to the days of old' and remembers how from the 'little town of Bethlehem' came the one who was to 'rule over Israel'.

It is a touching example of how bible reading is not merely recalling the past but a promise of the future. Isaiah pointed this out to the exiles in Babylon who tended to read the story of the Exodus as past: 'No need to recall the past, no need to think about what was done before. See, I am doing a new deed, even now it comes to light; can you not see it?' (Is 43:18-19). Jesus in the synagogue in Nazareth discovered his mission in the mission of Isaiah.

Micah's hope is not naïve. He recognises that Bethlehem's glory will not emerge immediately; they must go through a time of tribulation first, when God will appear to 'abandon' them. This is typical of biblical prophecy and very important for modern day prophets. There are no short cuts to glory; 'the grain of wheat must fall to the ground and die if it is to bear fruit'.

'The remnant of his brothers will come back to the sons of Israel.' Christian hope is always universal, never narrow in scope, never a matter of 'I will be saved' or 'you will be saved' but 'the whole of creation will be saved'. The greatness of God's people is not to be for their own sake, but for service, so that they can 'feed God's flock' which in our time we must understand as all of humanity.

We must understand 'he will stand' correctly. It speaks of self-confidence. God's people are self-possessed, they 'stand erect, their heads held high'. But they do not dominate, they serve. Similarly the 'power of the Lord' and 'the majesty of the name of God' are given to his people so that they may be instruments of his peace and that all men and women may be secure, even those who live at 'the ends of the land'.

The passage shows how mean and narrow is a Christian hope that remains focused on the church or even on the Christian family. Pope John Paul has challenged the church to reject the 'globalisation of individualism' and proclaim instead a 'globalisation of solidarity'. This is also the challenge of Micah's text.

Prayer

'India has nothing to fear from the church.' *Pope John Paul, visit to Asia, November 1999.*

Lord, forgive us followers of Jesus for attempting to limit your universal love, your power and the majesty of your name, which cause your sun to rise on bad as well as good, your rain to fall on honest and dishonest alike.

Broaden our minds so that we may stand confidently as followers of Jesus, share in his spirit of service, feed your flock in your power and in the majesty of your name, so that the human family may live securely, your love may be known to the ends of the land, and we may be your peace.

Lord, we thank you that you call us to serve the needy:
* those from other cultures;
* the homeless;
* addicts to drugs or alcohol;
* members of religious groups which are considered inferior.
Help us to come to them with respect:
* like Micah before the least of the clans of Judah;
* like Jesus when he ate with the tax collectors and prostitutes,
* like Paul preaching the good news to those who were far off.

In the eyes of society they are the least; help us to recognise that you have shared your creative power with them, and out of them will be born for you those who will rule over people, as has always been your plan, going back to the distant past, to the days of old.

At present their state is lowly, but that is temporary, the result of circumstances or perhaps of oppression; your glory has abandoned them for a brief time, their moment of grace will come and they whom you have destined to bring to birth something new and wonderful, will give birth.

They have been marginalised by society; they will come to their true identity as children of Israel, your chosen people.

They have been made to feel helpless, forever destined to beg favours from the wealthy and the powerful; they will have authority in the human family, will stand free and self-confident, and feed your flock with your power and the majesty of your name; they will extend their power to the ends of the earth. Far from being a burden to others, they themselves will be peace.

Lord, forgive us for offering false promises to people, holding out for them the hope of quick results. Give us the honesty of Micah and of Jesus to tell others that you will appear to abandon them until the time comes when she who is to give birth will give birth, that unless the grain of wheat falls on the ground and dies it remains only a single grain, but if it dies it yields a rich harvest.

Gospel Reading: Luke 1:39-44

39Mary set out and went as quickly as she could to a town in the hill country of Judah. 40She went into Zechariah's house and greeted Elizabeth. 41Now as soon as Elizabeth heard Mary's greeting, the child leapt in her womb and Elizabeth was filled with the Holy Spirit. 42She gave a loud cry and said, 'Of all women you are the most blessed, and blessed is the fruit of your womb. Why should I be honoured with a visit from the mother of my Lord? 43For the moment your greeting reached my ears, the child in my womb leapt for joy. 44Yes, blessed is she who believed that the promise made her by the Lord would be fulfilled.'

Meditation

Each year the gospel passage for this Sunday is a story of Mary's pregnancy, and for this year it is the visitation. We meditate on this story as the second joyful mystery of the rosary, so that this could be an opportunity to go into it deeper than we usually can in saying the rosary, and this would give depth to the way we say that prayer which plays an important part in the lives of many people.

It is the story of two pregnant women and, therefore, an opportunity to enter into the symbolism of that experience, especially for those who have gone through it, seeing it as a symbol of how waiting can be a creative time, one when we express our love and one also when we can unmask all the self-centredness that is latent within us and blocks our ability to give ourselves wholeheartedly to others. Of course, it could also be a meditation on the sacredness of pregnancy itself.

Mary should be the main focus of our attention, symbol at this moment of her life of the person of faith, and indeed of the church. Particularly significant is the expression 'blessed' that is attributed to her by Elizabeth; we must give the word its full biblical meaning, indicating that a person has a great gift from God and also that he or she has brought blessings to others. Mary's blessedness in this passage is simply that she has faith, no great achievements or visible signs of God's favour, just faith.

Prayer

Lord, there was a time when we had a dream:
* one day we would finally succeed in giving up drugs or drink and lead a healthy, creative life;
* we would develop a talent for music we knew we had but had never been recognised;
* we would be friends with someone we were too shy even to speak to;
* we would play our part in making our country a more human and caring place.

The dream was there within us but very small, so that people looking at us would think that we would never change. Then someone like Mary came into our lives, someone who also had a dream within her and so understood us. There was something in her greeting – not what she said – just the tone of her greeting as it reached our ears, and in an instant the dream within us came alive, like John the Baptist leaping for joy in the womb of Elizabeth. We felt confident that it would become a reality one day and we and the world would be different.

It was like being visited by a mother, not just an ordinary mother, but one who was giving birth to the presence of God. A deep feeling of humility came over us; we felt blessed and filled with the Holy Spirit.

Lord, we think today of some girl who is pregnant and regrets this pregnancy. Perhaps she has no one in the home to lean on; perhaps she is over-burdened with financial problems or finds that the child will block her career.

We ask you to send some Mary to visit her home, someone who has problems too but trusts that you will fulfil the hopes she has within her, and who will greet her in such a way that the child in her womb will leap for joy and she will feel blessed and filled with your Holy Spirit.

Lord, as a church, we have achievements that we are proud of, great resources too that others admire us for:
* schools that many parents want to send their children to;
* an international network from which we get encouragement and financial support;
* an ancient and highly respected spiritual tradition and a host of great saints whom we turn to as personal friends.
But all that can lead to being arrogant.

Help us rather to be like Mary, remembering that others have resources too, other churches, other faiths, other groups in society, so that we may visit them as Mary visited Elizabeth in the hill country, not with an ulterior motive or condescendingly, but just to greet them so that the moment the sound of our greeting reaches their ears they will rejoice in their gifts and in ours too.

Lord, there is a blessedness by which we experience great favours – when we pass an examination, get a promotion or overcome some bad habit. Help us to recognise the blessedness of Mary, that makes us the most blessed of all, when we trust that the promises you make us will be fulfilled. Great and wonderful things are born from that kind of blessedness.

Lord, we thank you for mothers in our country who had to struggle so hard to bring up their children well, and in spite of great odds have managed their homes with dignity. What kept them going was a faith like Mary's, the deep belief that you had planted certain convictions within them and that these would be vindicated. We have been blessed by having them among us, and many great people have been born as the fruit of their wombs.

HOW TO TRAIN YOUR DOG:

The *Right* Way & *Wrong* Way

Written by:
Gerri A. Larson

How To Train Your Dog: The Right Way and the Wrong Way

Copyright © 2015 Gerri A. Larson

ISBN-13: 978-1517345617
ISBN-10: 1517345618

Table of Contents

Introduction

Training a dog should not be a complex matter. It should not cause enormous stress to the pet owner. It should and could be fun!

If you are educated on the process, it would be like following a recipe or doing something over and over until mission accomplished by your canine; unfortunately, it usually turns out to be much more challenging than that and sometimes one of the biggest but most rewarding challenges in your life!

I have had 4 golden retrievers, 3 "unknowns," and 2 dachshunds in my life thus far and every one of them has all but run my life and I have spoiled them to the point where one might ask "who has trained who" and I think as you read on, the answer is quite obvious.

There are several things "to do" and "not to do" when training your dog. I will go through the top seven and hopefully this information will help you along the way when training your 4-legged family member. It may also save you hundreds of unnecessary hours of frustration and confusion.

I should tell you that I am not a professional trainer but I am a dog's best friend and their biggest fan. I can't even imagine my life without them.

Tip #1:

How to Greet Your Dog at the Door

It is very important to learn how to act when coming home (you-not the dog). Certainly, you are never to "flip out and go crazy." It is imperative for so many reasons that your dog is well behaved when you come home and open that door in order for that behavior to pass on to other guests that will someday hopefully visit you.   First impressions mean a lot!

You certainly do not want some classy guest that's all dressed up in very nice clean clothes to knock on your door with a pie in hand they had carefully chosen to bring for dessert and have your very untrained and misbehaving dog jump on that guest, getting their clothes dirty and even risking perhaps a raspberry pie dropping to the floor. Those are the kind of things to avoid when greeting guests.

Now, when I get home, I am probably more excited to see my dogs than they are to see me. I don't think about them in the morning so much but toward the middle of the afternoon, I start wondering what they are doing, if they are too warm, too cold, maybe sitting in the corner hovering because they really need to get out and pee but because they're so dedicated to me, they just suffer.

That is one of my incredibly sad thoughts I have during my day without them. I wonder if they are sleeping and if they have any idea that I might be running late. So by the time I'm just about home, I will admit I am very excited to see them again.

When I come dashing down our driveway, I hit the garage door opener and they, of course, can hear that wonderful noise. That means: "she's back!" I then try to get all my things together as quickly as I can and open the door. I always make sure my cell phone is in my purse and unplugged from the charger so I don't accidentally rip the dashboard off in my hurried attempts to flee out of the driver's seat like one would do on a burning plane. I then grab my coffee cup in hand from earlier in the day so I am ready to eject myself once the engine has stopped.

The extra time one takes to get things in order after stopping the engine is never a good idea; it is somewhat of a torturous feeling for the dog because they know you are on the other side of the door and it can truly drive them crazy! It builds up their anxiety as well as excitement.   Getting those little things done immediately after clicking the garage door opener is a much better idea!

I am then giddy with excitement.   I feel like "queen for the day."   I suddenly find myself speaking in a higher voice with sheer joy telling them how happy I am to be home.   They run through my legs, jump up and down and then I start jumping up and down and then they begin barking and howling quite loudly.   I am always pretty sure they're saying: *"Geez, we're so glad you're back; we love you so much; you still look great; I hope your day was good."*

It is quite the exhilarating feeling; that unconditional love will get you every time.

We then go downstairs and I take them outside. I habitually praise them and praise them some more about how fabulous they are because they can pee and poop! While I am doing this, I remember that I actually have to get to the bathroom myself but I "hold it" because I have my priorities in place.

They appear quite tickled about it as well. There are times when their tails actually wag in one full circle. This is quite incredible if I do say so myself. It is interesting to note that this circular wag is a sign of a dog with a very high IQ. All of my dogs have been able to accomplish this wag.

The entire event is probably 5 minutes or less but a great event at that.

Dog trainers will tell you that this ritual is the absolute worst thing you can do. Firstly and of extreme importance, you never **ever** act like you're happy when you get home. You are supposed to act like you've had a lobotomy and are basically "just passing through."

You open the door after taking your good old time in the car collecting items, perhaps even reading the mail in your car that you just pulled out of your mailbox before coming down the driveway, maybe even calling your credit card company to dispute a charge you've just noticed on your statement, maybe even reviewing a few text messages when the engine has stopped because you know you're not supposed to do that while driving.

You do all this because you know that you are a proper dog owner and you are the boss and there should be no "rush" to get inside. You are always in charge.

You should act like you don't even "THINK" they are home and you have not thought about them all day. When you walked out of that door 9 hours ago, it was truly "out of sight-out of mind."

Upon opening the door, you simply say "hi" to them like you were just gone for a moment and then you take off your coat and casually hang it up, again, not being in any hurry whatsoever.

It is ok to say "good dog" after they have gone outside and have successfully done their "business" but you certainly don't need to jump up and down like a cheerleader and act like they've just saved a child's life. That is not appropriate. It is wildly inappropriate and uncalled for.

After telling your dog that he/she is "good" in a very semi-monotone fashion, it is then and only then that you are to pet them and give them the loving they so deserve.   They are hungry and starving at this point for love and attention; that is the way it should be.

In this fashion, they will acknowledge who is boss and learn how to appropriately meet you as well as guests when they enter your home.

Tip #2:

Training Your Dog to be Quiet During

Phone Conversations

You may be thinking this isn't really a huge training tip but I consider it to be one of the most important. If you already have a dog and a phone, you most likely already understand why this is so imperative.

My dogs, for some peculiar reason, find it very threatening emotionally when I am on the phone.

That has become somewhat of a problem for me that I've had to adapt to and adjust and re-adjust time and time again.

Dogs need to learn they are not in charge of the home, the homeowner and certainly not the phone! This also includes when the owner is engaged in any type of phone conversation.

When the phone rings, it is most likely not someone calling to speak to your dog. Therefore, it is incredibly rude and inappropriate for your dog to "take over the conversation."

Your dog may tend to react differently when the phone rings and you will find yourself adjusting to this behavior simply to complete a phone call.

I have never had the pleasure of a relaxing phone call when my dogs are around. They immediately either jump off the floor and start barking or come over to the phone and start barking very loudly and rudely into my phone and any and all conversations are then seriously compromised, to say the least.

Typically, 50% of my calls are business and the other half are my friends discussing their day. Either way, it's hard for individuals on the other end to carry on any type of connected thoughts with dogs literally screaming in the background and, of course, me telling them to be quiet.

I've adjusted in my own way and it is not something I recommend to you but I'll share it in case there is an unforeseen emergency and your dog simply will not remain quiet.

The first step is to immediately "stand up." This quick movement startles the dog and they know that something is going to happen. Typically, it is something in their favor. For very important phone calls, I immediately go to the "treat jar" and throw treats non-stop. This will keep your dog busy and totally occupied eating the treats and will almost guarantee cessation in barking. When the treats are gone or when you've realized they've consumed too many calories in a one minute period and the conversation must continue, you can then go into your shower. The shower has proven to be a very effective place to take care of important business calls. You should not turn "on" the shower but certainly shut the shower door in order for your dog to think you are truly unavailable. This technique works every time because most dogs will then believe their owner is washing themselves and simply singing a tune. Your dog will then not even think about barking or asking for another treat as they will understand that you are cleaning yourself and dogs do have a good understanding and respect for that.

Dog trainers will never recommend owners "jumping into a shower" or "flooding your pet with treats."

When a dog hears a phone ring, a dog trainer will be more than adamant about your dog knowing immediately that a ringing phone means a quiet dog.

You should never have to worry in your own home about speaking on the phone and having noisy dogs in the background.

The well trained dog will look at you getting ready to pick up the phone and once the owner says "*shh*," the dog immediately turns his head and lies down. The "*shh*" noise is something a professional dog trainer does and it supposedly "mesmerizes" the dog and they immediately want to take a nap. The well trained dog should always know that the phone call is never for them and they should not get involved.

If you can accomplish this, you can be assured you will never have to take business calls in the shower.

Tip #3:

Training Your Dog to Sleep on the Floor

Dogs are not human beings and should not sleep in your bed. This has been another hard one for me to comprehend. I recently purchased a king sized bed because of my two healthy golden retrievers and their love of stretching out and wanting their bellies rubbed in the middle of the night.

Initially, I would get into the bed and try sleeping on the right hand side. One dog typically sleeps on the bottom and the other dog sleeps on the floor for approximately 10 minutes. For the time being, I find myself very comfortable. After that time, my retriever lying on the floor will sit up and just start staring at me. He sometimes clears his throat in kind of a "fake" way but letting me know he's there in case I've dozed off. He wants to sleep on the right side of the bed and he wants me to get my pillows and me out of his way so he can make it with one jump. If I'm really tired or just feeling too lazy at the moment to move, I pretend I am sleeping and do not make any unnecessary movements, especially with my eyes because he is always looking directly at me. I lie still hoping that he will think I'm truly asleep and just go lie down and be happy where he is. He then clears his throat again and I become incredibly guilty and feel terrible about myself.

Dogs will try to make you feel bad about yourself; it helps them get what they want. It usually works.

I then roll over, move the pillows, adjust the blankets and let my other dog up. I make sure he is comfortable and he stretches out and takes up more than half of the bed and I am curled up then on the left side, on the very edge and hoping the phone does not ring because it's on his side.

Dog trainers always recommend that a forceful "*now go to bed*" spoken and direct eye contact to let them know you are definitely not kidding should take care of it and a well-behaved dog will then immediately drop to the floor.

The properly trained dog will learn to lie down by their owners and sleep through the night. They will think about the next day to come and when 3 a.m. rolls around and they need to go outside, they will simply "hold it" because they've been trained to do so. They will lie still and make only minimal noises while they are dreaming because even the most well behaved dog cannot control their dreams and most dog owners will not spend money on psychoanalysis.

Tip #4:

Training Your Dog to go on Walks Correctly

There is a very concrete way to walk a dog correctly. In dog training 101, everyone knows that dogs should always remain at your side and nowhere else.   It is imperative that a dog do this to enjoy his walk as well as the owner's walk.   You will see well behaved dogs walking with their owner while the owner is sometimes comfortably reading a book, talking on the phone, trimming his mustache, and perhaps even grading papers.

The well behaved dog is never a problem and the owner sometimes even forgets there is a dog attached to the leash.

A dog should never be ahead of the owner and be "pulling" on a leash as so many badly trained dogs do.

I have never been able to master this art.   I believe that is why I have back pain from my spine being out of alignment for the past twenty years.   I have seen dogs literally walking next to their owner without a leash on and I've wondered if there was something like an "invisible leash" like "invisible braces" people have on their teeth.   It's been nothing short of a mystery for me to witness. It is actually a miracle.

Owners should remain very confident in walking their dogs and not be concerned of other dogs coming their way.

I have had many nightmares about killer dogs or even a bear hiding in the woods jumping on my helpless dependent and needy creatures and literally eating them up in the daylight in front of me. For that reason, I have had to come up with a solution in adapting for survival in the event of an emergency.

I have learned to immediately do one of two things when seeing any animal approach.

My first approach is to drop down and "tent myself" over my dogs as though I am trying to suffocate them when in reality I am responding as a human shield.

My second approach is to yank their leashes and run wildly in the opposite direction. My dogs are accustomed to this type of fear and have actually learned how to trot like horses in unison ahead of me in our attempts of fleeing from a possible life-threatening situation and happily avoiding the tearing up of body parts, mine and theirs.

We run until we cannot see any animals and then find our car and go home. I often feel like Dorothy after she clicked her heels 3 times and found out she was safe again. It's a brilliant feeling to have my dogs safe, we get a little exercise for the day and we are home free! Treats are ample and justified after the vigorous work-out, physically and mentally. As a dog owner, I too participate in a treat, as I feel I could have very well just saved a few doggy-lives!

In both of these approaches it is interesting to note that other dog walkers will observe and be frightened of you as well and want to run away from you with their dogs. This helps all parties.

This is the incorrect strategy for dog walking. Fear should never be even a "thought" during your walk.

The well trained dog will always be at your side. The dog will never run ahead of you or behind you because a stern look as taught by the professional dog trainer will be enough to keep the dog directly at your side. The dog will then realize the simple joy of walking at your side and have no plans whatsoever of straying. The leash in this case with such a brilliantly trained dog is truly an after-thought and a cosmetic item for show.

The well trained dog is not frightened or threatened by other dogs. They will walk past a dog, nod to say "hello" and then keep going. They will want to sniff their butts but they will know this is highly inappropriate, especially in a public setting. They may sniff lightly while passing by the other dog but will do it in a secret way that dogs do, so as not to be rude. The highly trained dog is always a joy to walk with.

Tip #5:

Training Your Dog to Behave at Meal Time

Most rational human beings understand that dogs have their food and you have your food and that's the way it should be.

The majority of veterinarians and pet professionals will tell you that "table scraps" are never a good idea. They are better suited for leftovers or the garbage disposal.

Dogs eat their food and you eat yours! This is a simple fact but hard to do for millions of dog owners.

When I am preparing supper, I have dogs directly beneath me. It's nice to have someone around but I know why they are there and I'd much rather they go into the other room and watch Animal Planet or get the weather report for the next day in case we had the courage to venture out for a walk but they are simply unable to leave my side.

Like any good cook, I always try to sample along the way to assure the taste is "just right." I have a hard time not sharing because I was raised to believe that sharing is the right thing to do and subsequently find myself allowing my dogs to taste-test as well.

They always seem to give me a "thumbs up" with everything I cook and appear so incredibly impressed with the taste of every bite. I have to say in all honesty, because of this, I have felt more than once as though I may have the capability of becoming an international chef. They smile throughout the taste testing and I cannot remember a meal that wasn't a 5 star hit for them as far as smiles, head nods and paws wanting to do a "high five" after jumping on the counter. It is a positive experience all the way around.

Sadly, a well-trained dog should stay out of the kitchen. There are really no exceptions to this rule.

The supper table rules are very similar to the kitchen rules. Dogs should stay away from the supper table as well when the meal is being served.

This simply becomes torture to dogs when needing to simply lie still around large amounts of gourmet food and often times promotes bad behaviors. This could possibly be due to repressed feelings coming to the forefront. Dogs have been known to dream predominantly about food and the lack of. These dreams/nightmares are very sad and frightening and sitting under a table or across a room watching people eat and stuffing their mouths can put a dog into "mini crisis."

Dog trainers will tell you explicitly that a dog at the supper table is not appropriate and they should be "seen but not heard." This phrase, I believe, was created back in the 60's for children, probably for me; I didn't like it then and I don't like it now.

Tip #6:

Training Your Dog to Learn

Commands

Professional dog trainers believe that dogs can have a good working vocabulary if trained appropriately. They believe the majority of dogs have been known to have 125-200 words that they become familiar with during their life time.

As far as commands, it varies but trainers contend that dogs can learn up to 25, sometimes more, depending on the dog's IQ.

I have never counted the number of words my dogs have in their vocabulary but I believe it is in the thousands. As far as commands, it is endless.

A good dog trainer will train a dog with commands spoken over and over until memorized. Upon learning them, they get a little "beep" from a horn or a .000000001 ounce doggy treat. The doggy treats have no substantive value and the dogs are very aware of this. A well trained dog will take it nonetheless because the dog is sensitive and caring enough to believe that the owner will be hurt if they don't eat it.

I have never been able to train my dog in words but rather sentences and "if-then" scenarios. They seem to have grasped on to that much easier and efficiently and coupled with my numerous expressions of gratitude, it has worked for me.

"If you go inside right now and you are a good boy we will watch Animal Planet and I will make a meatloaf." In this one command, there are more than 20 words stated to my dog. I probably have more than 500 of these so you can see how many words my dogs must have learned vs. the average dog and I'm not even a professional dog trainer.

A professional dog trainer will instruct you to give "short commands" in order for rapid memorization. "Sit doggy." This is often accompanied by a hand going down slowly so the dog knows to move its way to the floor. My dogs know what "*sit*" means and I have never actually had to draw my hand down; I simply tell them to "sit down if they want to go outside and play later and then get a snack" and they totally understand that. These are two very different methods of training.

I believe the professional dog trainers will tell you that I am doing this inappropriately.

A professional dog trainer will help you with short commands and they will also give you comfort in telling you that you dog will be able to learn several over time. Dog trainers are full of hope.

It's up to you how you want to go about this sometimes confusing process, learning short commands vs. long detailed sentences. This should always be a serious consideration. It also depends on your dog's IQ and you will eventually be able to figure this out as well.

Tip #7:

Training Your Dog to Share

Training a dog to share is very difficult, if not impossible. Why do you need to teach your dog to share, anyway? I've heard so many people ask this question and they truly believe that it is important to teach "sharing" to their dog. For this reason and this reason only, I have included it in my tips.

A professional dog trainer is good in this regard as they do not have any opinions either way about the possibility of a dog "not being able to share."

A dog trainer will tell you that all dogs can learn to share. For example, they might work on bowls of dog food sitting idle until the owner sits down with them and then allocates portions. I'm not sure what the benefit of this is but humans for some reason find it important to teach this to their dog. It has been my experience that humans learn to share and dogs do not.

I have been very lack in training my dogs to share because of my belief system and have opted to simply give them their own spaces, individual dog dishes, individual dog toys and when dispensing snacks or treats, give evenly across the board.

Consider the following scenario. You are having a dinner party and sitting at the dining table laughing and eating bread and drinking wine. There is an abundance of food around you and everyone appears to be happy. Your dogs are watching you and the guests. You may have had a "sharing lesson" earlier in the day and while it was quite boring for the dogs, they listened anyway because they love you and didn't want to appear to have a bad attitude. And then the party begins and while the people are eating, which appears to be a lot of food, no one is sharing anything with your dogs. They are sitting with their heads to the floor wondering why the sharing has stopped for them. Hardly seems fair, right?

Dogs are not able to compartmentalize their training to be applicable in only some situations. They are not wired in that way. That is one of several reasons that I do not teach my dogs to share.

If you have a dog that shares I think that is wonderful. I'm not sure how it happened, but kudos to you!

LOVING YOUR DOG

Of course, no tips needed here.

A professional dog trainer or veterinarian might tell you to always keep things in perspective and to remember that a dog is an animal and not a human being. Now, that's just silly, isn't it? I can tell you that I cannot imagine a world without dogs. If you have one, you know what I'm talking about.

Loving a dog and getting that unconditional love back is one of the purest and greatest gifts in life!

Enjoy your pet.

Don't sweat the small stuff.

Lucky lucky you!

Happy trails my friend!

Gerri Larson

13670198R00026

Printed in Great Britain
by Amazon.co.uk, Ltd.,
Marston Gate.